BIOGRAPHY FROM
ANCIENT CIVILIZATIONS
LEGENDS, FOLKLORE, AND STORIES OF ANCIENT WORLDS

The Life and Times of
CLOVIS, KING OF THE FRANKS

Mitchell Lane
PUBLISHERS
P.O. Box 196
Hockessin, Delaware 19707
www.mitchelllane.com

TITLES IN THE SERIES

The Life and Times of

BIOGRAPHY FROM
ANCIENT CIVILIZATIONS
LEGENDS, FOLKLORE, AND STORIES OF ANCIENT WORLDS

The Life and Times of

CLOVIS,
KING OF THE FRANKS

Earle Rice, Jr.

Mitchell Lane
PUBLISHERS

Printing   1   2   3   4   5   6   7   8   9

Library of Congress Cataloging-in-Publication Data
Rice, Earle.
  The life and times of Clovis / by Earle Rice Jr.
      p. cm.—(Biography from ancient civilizations) (The life and times of)
  Includes bibliographical references and index.
  ISBN 978-1-58415-742-7 (library bound)
  1. Clovis, King of the Franks, ca. 466–511—Juvenile literature. 2. France—Kings and rulers—Biography—Juvenile literature. 3. France—History—To 987—Juvenile literature. I. Title.
  DC67.R535 2010
  944'.013092—dc22
  [B]

                                                                    2009027364

ABOUT THE AUTHOR: Earle Rice Jr. is a former senior design engineer and technical writer in the aerospace, electronic-defense, and nuclear industries. He has devoted full time to his writing since 1993 and is the author of more than fifty published books. Earle is listed in *Who's Who in America* and is a member of the Society of Children's Book Writers and Illustrators, the League of World War I Aviation Historians, the Air Force Association, and the Disabled American Veterans.

PUBLISHER'S NOTE: This story is based on the author's extensive research, which he believes to be accurate. Documentation of such research is contained on page 46.

The internet sites referenced herein were active as of the publication date. Due to the fleeting nature of some web sites, we cannot guarantee they will all be active when you are reading this book.

To reflect current usage, we have chosen to use the secular era designations BCE ("before the common era") and CE ("of the common era") instead of the traditional designations BC ("before Christ") and AD (*anno Domini*, "in the year of the Lord").

CONTENTS

                    *For Your Information

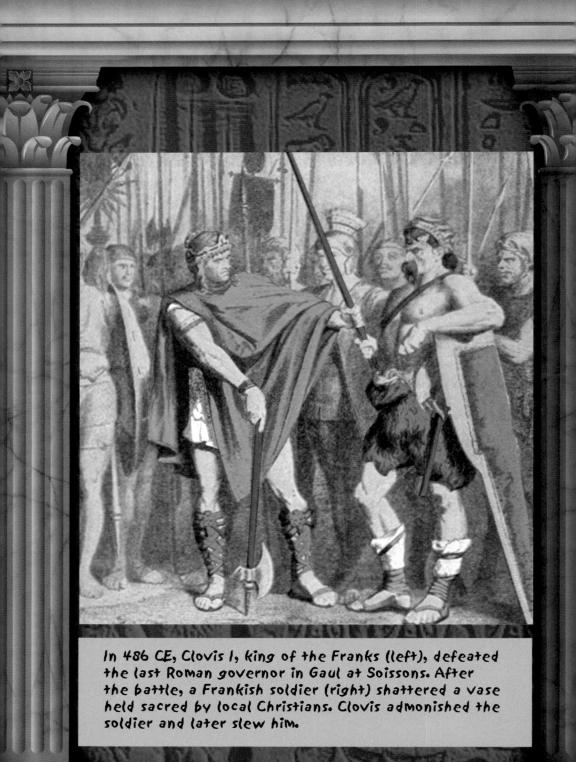

In 486 CE, Clovis I, king of the Franks (left), defeated the last Roman governor in Gaul at Soissons. After the battle, a Frankish soldier (right) shattered a vase held sacred by local Christians. Clovis admonished the soldier and later slew him.

CHAPTER
ONE

"A GREAT AND DISTINGUISHED WARRIOR"

Rome fell in the last quarter of the fifth century. Much of its steadying influence in Western Europe gave way to the rise and sweep of pagan tribes and barbarians. It was a time of fierce warriors and fiercer kings. Christianity and the refinements of a civilized society came under attack by hordes of wild-eyed heathens. Their battle-axes and short swords savagely chopped and slashed away at the glory that once was Rome. Clerics fell to their blades, and churches were desecrated. The pagan hordes held nothing sacred.

In the year 486 CE, a particularly savage band of barbarians sacked a church near Soissons (swah-SOHN) in Gaul (now France). They carried off all the ornaments of the holy ministry. Among their booty was, in the words of Gregory of Tours, "a vase of marvelous size and beauty."[1] (Gregory was the bishop of Tours. He wrote a history of the era, which preserved much of what is known today about that time and place.) Afterward, the bishop of that church sent a plea to the king and leader of the looters. His message implored the heathen king to return the goods— if not all the holy vessels, then at least the valued vase.

In response, the heathen king bade the bishop's messenger to accompany him to Soissons, where the loot was to be divided. "If the lot [his warrior band] shall give me this vase," he said, "I will do what the bishop desires."[2] So the messenger went along.

At Soissons, the king asked his men to grant him the vase in question in addition to his rightful share of the booty. Reasonable men among his band replied in unison: "O glorious king, all things which we see are thine, and we ourselves are subject to thy power; now do what seems pleasing to thee, for none is strong enough to resist thee."[3] Despite the agreed consent of most, the voice of one of the king's soldiers rose in dissent.

Gregory of Tours described the soldier as "impetuous, envious, and vain."[4] Raising his battle-ax high, he shattered the vase with a powerful downward blow, crying, "Thou shalt receive nothing of this unless a just lot give it to thee."[5] His rash declaration stunned the others into silence. They looked to their king, who was known for his patience. He showed no outward sign of emotion, but a wound began to fester in his heart. Several soldiers of more moderate temperament gathered up the shattered pieces of the once-beautiful vase. The king handed them to the bishop's messenger and sent him on his way. Most witnesses to the incident soon forgot about it. The king did not.

After a year had passed, the king assembled his army to display their arms on the *Campus Martius* ("Field of Mars"), a broad, open area outside the city of Tournai (tur-NAY; now in Belgium). While reviewing his warriors, he came to the brash soldier who had smashed the vase to pieces. He liked little of what he saw. Nothing the soldier did would have pleased him. "No one bears his arms so clumsily as thou," he admonished the impetuous one, "for neither thy spear, nor thy sword, nor thy ax is ready for use."[6] He seized the soldier's ax and cast it upon the ground. When the soldier stooped to pick it up, the king cleaved his head with a lethal blow from his own ax. "Thus," he said, "didst thou to the vase at Soissons."[7]

Shattering the sacred vase

This happened in March of 487. It was a time of fierce warriors and fiercer kings. And no king was fiercer than Clovis, king of the Franks.

The Franks first appeared in the pages of recorded history in the third century CE. A Germanic-speaking barbarian tribe, they lived on the east bank of the middle and lower Rhine River. Basically, three tribal branches existed at that time—the Salians, the Ripuarians, and the Chatti (or Hessians). Language and customs formed a common bond among the three branches, but each was governed independently.

Collectively, the Franks later evoked both praise and criticism from Edward Gibbon, author of *The Decline and Fall of the Roman Empire.* "They deserved, they assumed, they maintained the honourable epithet of Franks or Freemen,"[8] he wrote. But he also pointed out that an "inconstant spirit, the thirst of rapine [pillaging], and a disregard to the most solemn treaties disgraced the character of the Franks."[9] Despite these flaws, they would give rise to two of Europe's great nations.

About the mid-200s, the Franks set out on their great European adventure. From their homelands in the Rhine Valley, they began to infiltrate and settle inside the frontier of the Western Roman Empire near Mainz (MYNTZ) in present-day western Germany. In 276, West Roman legions under Probus, one of several "restorer" emperors, forced them back across the Rhine. After several victories over the Franks, Probus reported to his senate: "[W]e have slain four thousand of the enemy; we have had offered to us sixteen thousand men ready armed; and we have wrested from the enemy the seventy most important towns. The Gauls, in fact, are completely delivered."[10] (Ancient Gaul occupied the region that covers most of modern-day France and Belgium and parts of the Netherlands, Luxembourg, Germany, and Switzerland.) Probus then began the restoration of civilian communities that barbarian tribes had been ravaging for the past four decades.

Eighty-two years later, in 358 CE, Emperor Julian besieged and defeated a band of some six hundred Salian Franks in a castle on the Meuse River. Forsaking an ancient creed that bade them to conquer or to fight to the death, the Franks surrendered to Julian's West Roman legions after fifty-seven days. Julian, magnanimous in victory, later permitted the Franks to settle as subjects of the empire in the region between the

Meuse and Scheldt rivers known then as Toxandria. Many of them joined the imperial army as auxiliaries. Some helped to guard the Roman frontier as *foederati* (federated allies). Such services perpetuated a long association with the Romans that had begun under Probus.

At that time, the Salian Franks were divided into several groups. A chief or *regulus* (plural *reguli*) headed each group. Among these groups, the Merovingians (mehr-uh-VIN-jee-uns) emerged as the dominant one. The Merovingians took their name from a chief named Merovech (probably meaning "Son of the Sea"). History recalls him only as the father of his successor, Childeric I, who ruled the Salian Franks from his capital at Tournai. Under Merovech and Childeric, the Salians extended their domain, some say as far south as the Somme River.

Childeric remained a loyal ally of the West Romans until the death of Emperor Majorian in 461 CE. About that time, Childeric's subjects seized his throne and banished him to Thuringia (thur-IN-jee-uh; now a state in central Germany) for dishonoring a number of Salian maidens. Before his departure, he left a trusted friend in charge. His friend divided a gold piece and gave half of it to Childeric. He promised to send his matching half of the coin to the king when it became safe for Childeric to return to Tournai. Childeric spent the next several years in exile with Basinus and Basina, the king and queen of Thuringia. Soon after he left, the Franks selected Aegidius (ee-JID-ee-us), the Roman military commander, as their new king.

Eight years passed. Childeric's loyal friend finally won back the people's good will. He sent his half of the divided gold piece to Childeric as a sign that his people wanted him back. Childeric returned to Tournai, and the Salian Franks restored him to his kingdom. Not long afterward, Basina left her husband and showed up at Childeric's court in Tournai. Surprised, Childeric asked her why she had journeyed so far to see him. "I know your worth," she replied, "and that you are very strong, and therefore I have come to live with you. For let me tell you that if I had known of any one more worthy than you in parts beyond the sea I should certainly have sought to live with him."[11] Basina's affection for him pleased him greatly, and he married her.

"And she conceived and bore a son and called his name Clovis," wrote Gregory of Tours. "He was a great and distinguished warrior."[12]

Gregory of Tours

What the world knows today about Clovis and the sixth-century Gallo-Roman kingdom, it owes almost exclusively to the writings of Gregory of Tours (TOOR). Gregory was born to a family of aristocrats in 538 or 539 in Clermont in Auvergne (oh-VERN) in what is now France. He was originally named Georgius Florentius. His family supplied several bishops in central Gaul (France), including Gregory, who succeeded his cousin as bishop of Tours in 573.

Tours stood on the Loire River and the main thoroughfare between Spain and Aquitaine (AK-wih-tayn) and the north. It also formed the hub of five Roman roads. Because of its central location, most of the important people of the time either visited or passed through it at one time or another. More important, the influence of the Franks in the north and the Romans in the south met at Tours. Gregory could find few better places from which to scribe the history of his time.

Gregory's role as bishop involved him in numerous political controversies. He often criticized Chilperic I, the grandson of Clovis, for his depraved conduct and cruel treatment of his subjects. His open conflict with the king led to his trial and acquittal for slandering Fredegund, Chilperic's queen, in 580. More positively, Gregory actively promoted cults of various saints and restored many churches in his diocese. But his claim to fame came not from his religious pursuits but rather from his writings.

Gregory wrote seven books of miracles, and portrayed the lives of saints in *Lives of the Fathers*. Apart from his religious works, however, his masterwork was *Ten Books of History*, more popularly known as *The History of the Franks*. Critics have been quick to point out many grammatical and structural flaws in his *History*. In his preface, Gregory himself asked his readers to bear with him "should I violate the laws of grammar to a serious or minor degree, since I have not been well schooled in that subject."[13] Flaws and all, Gregory's *History* provides fascinating insight into the world of the Franks that would otherwise have gone unrecorded.

Gregory of Tours

Clovis I, pictured in *Clovis roi des Francs* (*Clovis king of the Franks*) by François-Louis Dejuinne (1786–1844), gazes with uncommon intensity from out of the past. A fierce warrior and a wise ruler, he succeeded in uniting all of the Franks by force and by guile.

BIOGRAPHY FROM

ANCIENT CIVILIZATIONS

LEGENDS, FOLKLORE, AND STORIES OF ANCIENT WORLDS

CHAPTER
TWO

KING OF THE SALIAN FRANKS

History offers only the barest glimpse of Childeric's life and reign as king of the Salian Franks. Again, Gregory of Tours provides what little information about him that has survived. Unfortunately, later scholars have questioned the accuracy of much of Gregory's historical writings. Some believe that the Franks did not *elect* Aegidius to rule during Childeric's exile to Thuringia. They instead suggest that Aegidius more likely took back the Roman lands occupied earlier by the Franks by force. He was, after all, the West Roman *magister militum* ("master of the soldiers") in Gaul.

To explain why Aegidius stepped down graciously as the Frankish ruler, Edward Gibbon wrote: "[H]is vanity rather than his ambition was gratified by that singular honour"[1] of being *elected* as king. Thus, upon Childeric's return from exile, Aegidius "patiently acquiesced in the restoration of the lawful prince."[2] Gibbon must have imagined this explanation. Gregory of Tours recorded no such details. All that is known for sure is that Childeric somehow recovered his kingship and continued in the service of the Romans.

Childeric and his Franks afterward joined in Aegidius's victory over the Visigoths near Orléans in 463. (The Visigoths were a Germanic tribe that had settled in southern Gaul.) At about that time, a plague fell over the land and killed many people. The dead included Aegidius. He left a son named Syagrius (sy-AG-ree-us). In 469, Childeric helped Count

Paulus, Aegidius's successor, to withstand further Visigoth incursions into Gaul. He then assisted Paulus in clearing Saxon invaders led by Odoacer (oh-doh-AY-sur) from the region southwest of Orléans around Angers (an-ZHAY). Childeric's successful defense of Angers defeated Odoacer and forced the Germanic leader into Roman service.

According to Gregory of Tours, Childeric slew Count Paulus during his defense of the city. More likely, Paulus was slain by the Saxons. In any case, "the Saxons fled and left many of their people to be slain, the Romans pursuing,"[3] noted Gregory. Later, Odoacer struck an alliance with Childeric. Together, they turned back the Alemanni, a Germanic people who had overrun part of Italy. Odoacer went on to overthrow Romulus Augustulus (ROM-yuh-lus aw-GUS-tuh-lus), the last Western Roman emperor.

Odoacer's conquest marked the fall of the Western Roman Empire in 476. He became the first barbarian king of Italy. Childeric apparently hung up his sword after the Italian campaign and died of natural causes in 481. His tomb was discovered at Tournai in 1653. It contained the remains of his royal cloak, his arms, and many gold ornaments.

Clovis succeeded Childeric as king of the Salian Franks at the age of fifteen. Gregory offered no physical description of the young king. Of the transition, Gregory simply stated: "Childeric died and Clovis his son reigned in his stead."[4] Clovis took on responsibilities that would awe a seasoned monarch, but he carried himself like a man born to be king. "When he first took the field," wrote Edward Gibbon, "he had neither gold and silver in his coffers, nor wine and corn in his magazines [storehouses]; but he imitated the example of Caesar [SEE-zhar], who in the same country had acquired wealth by the sword, and purchased soldiers with the fruits of conquest."[5]

When Clovis became king, the Salian Franks occupied the region around Tournai in present-day Belgium. During his thirty-year reign, he would expand his Frankish kingdom to cover most of Gaul; he would unite all the Franks into a single powerful nation; and he would lend variations of his name to at least twenty-five future European rulers and one Holy Roman emperor. Variations of the name Clovis include Chlodwig and Ludvig (German), Lewis (English), and Louis (French).

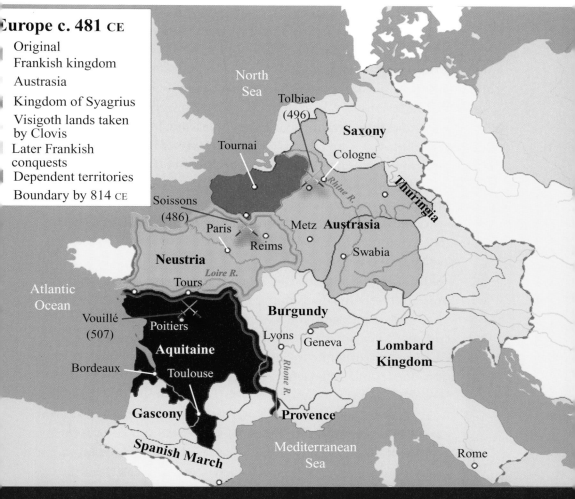

Europe c. 481 CE

- Original Frankish kingdom
- Austrasia
- Kingdom of Syagrius
- Visigoth lands taken by Clovis
- Later Frankish conquests
- Dependent territories
- Boundary by 814 CE

North Sea

Tolbiac (496)

Saxony

Tournai

Cologne

Rhine R.

Thuringia

Soissons (486)

Paris

Metz   **Austrasia**

Reims

Swabia

Neustria

Loire R.

Atlantic Ocean

Tours

Vouillé (507)

Poitiers

Burgundy

Lyons   Geneva

Lombard Kingdom

Aquitaine

Bordeaux

Toulouse

Rhone R.

Gascony

Provence

Spanish March

Mediterranean Sea

Rome

Clovis was one of several Frankish kings in northwestern Gaul and the Rhineland. In 486, he began a campaign of expansion with his defeat of Syagrius, the last Roman governor in Gaul. He continued his conquests with victories over the Thuringians, Alemanni, Burgundians, and Visigoths.

Despite the fall of the Western Roman Empire in 476, Clovis found his first challenge in the continuing Roman presence in Gaul.

After the deaths of Aegidius and Count Paulus, the Roman interests in Gaul were represented by Syagrius. His official title is obscure, but he answered to Zeno, the East Roman emperor in Constantinople. (The

Roman Empire split into East and West divisions in 395 CE.) Because the Franks regarded the Roman-held territory as a kingdom, they referred to Syagrius as "king of the Romans." More accurately, he served as the military governor of Roman Gaul. Despite the long-standing Frankish history of Roman service, the Roman presence in Gaul did not fit well with the ambitions of Clovis.

At that time, Syagrius governed the Roman district from his seat in Soissons. Clovis, who wanted to recover lands once ruled by his kinsmen, rebelled against Roman rule in northern Gaul. He sent a defiant message to Syagrius, inviting him to appoint a time and a place for their respective armies to meet. The contested ownership of Soissons and surrounding territories would be decided in the manner of most medieval land disputes—by the sword. In the words of Edward Gibbon, "Syagrius received, and boldly accepted, the hostile defiance of Clovis."[6] He soon found cause to regret his decision.

Clovis prepared for war. He enlisted the aid of two of his cousins. They were lesser kings named Ragnachar and Chararic. (There were other kings among the Salian Franks, but Clovis was dominant.) Ragnachar reigned over the Cambrai (kam-BRAY) Franks; Chararic ruled the Tongres (tohn-JUH) Franks.

Clovis moved against Syagrius in 486. Their armies clashed at Soissons on the Loire River. In the battle of Soissons, the ax-throwing Franks crushed the loose band of Roman volunteers and mercenaries that opposed them. Syagrius fled from the battlefield to seek refuge in the court of Alaric II, king of the Visigoths, at Toulouse (too-LOOZ).

Clovis sent word to Alaric to return Syagrius to him at Soissons. A fearful Alaric had no wish to anger Clovis. He readily surrendered Syagrius in chains to Frankish agents. Upon their return to Soissons, Clovis ordered the beheading of Syagrius. Soon afterward, he cleaved the head of the soldier who had shattered the bishop's precious vase. After victory on the field of battle and revenge on the Field of Mars, Clovis firmly established (or reestablished) the Merovingian dynasty over all of Gaul between the Somme and Loire rivers. In

Scramasax

addition to Soissons, his expanded realm now included the surrounding Roman region of Belgica Secunda (BEL-jih-kuh say-KUN-duh). At age twenty, Clovis had shown himself to be a fearsome leader. And he was just getting started.

Clovis owed the ease of his conquests in large part to the help of the Catholic hierarchy and the clergy of Gaul. Although a pagan himself, the wily Clovis must have recognized the value of having the church on his side when battling his heathen or Arian adversaries, such as the Visigoths, Ostrogoths, and Burgundians. (Heathens worshiped no god or many gods; Arians believed that God alone is God, and that there is no unity of Father, Son, and Holy Spirit in a single Godhead.) Clovis cultivated harmonious relations with the clergy for good reason: He needed all the help he could get to accomplish his ambitious aims. As a young king, however, Clovis displayed less than god-fearing traits. Joseph Dahmus, a specialist in medieval history, characterized Clovis in forthright terms: "[H]is level of moral development appears to have been no higher than that of his semicivilized neighbors. He was as savage and treacherous as they were, although more cunning and ambitious. He displayed his savagery by eliminating, by means mostly foul, all who opposed him in his quest for power, or whose lands he coveted, whether they were friends, relatives, or enemies."[7]

Traditionally, violent men rule violently in violent times. Clovis proved the rule. Violence and brutality demonstrably formed a part of his nature. As with most men who rise to greatness, however, there were many redeeming facets to his character. Certainly none can fault his courage. Nor can anyone deny the discipline and order he brought to a world populated by free-spirited barbarians. At his command,

Francisca

Kingdoms at the Time of Clovis' Death, 511 CE

North Sea

Britain

Atlantic Ocean

English Channel

Saxons

Bretons

Tournai

Reims

Thuringians

Paris

Dijon

Kingdom of the Franks

Tours

Orleans

Alemanni

Slovenes

Bavarians

Ostrogoths

Bordeaux

Burgundians

Clermont

Toulouse

Lombards

Visigoths

Mediterranean Sea

Adriatic Sea

Clovis I ruled the Franks for three decades. He led his barbarian armies on a series of forays into Gallo-Roman and Burgundian lands in the southeast and Visigothic territory in the southwest. His conquests profoundly altered the face of Western Europe.

his armies passed through peaceful lands treading lightly, turning not so much as a blade of grass that might disturb the calm or defile the region. His justice was swift but fair; his punishment, instant death.

"In all his transactions with mankind," observed Edward Gibbon, "he calculated the weight of interest, of passion, and of opinion; and his measures were sometimes adapted to the sanguinary [bloody] manners of the Germans, and sometimes moderated by the milder genius of Rome and Christianity."[8] He was a man of his times, a man for all seasons. He was Clovis, king of the Salian Franks.

Franks in Action

By the time Clovis appeared on the European scene, the Franks had fought both with and against the Romans for many years. Rome owed its glory to legions of well-armed and well-equipped fighting men. Highly disciplined and superbly led, they carved an empire that stretched from the British Isles to the Middle East. Surprisingly, the Franks seem to have borrowed nothing in the way of weapons and armor from their Roman contemporaries. In Clovis's time, they went into action bareheaded, lightly shielded, and simply armed.

Franks entered battle wearing only a tight-fitting, short-skirted linen tunic (outer garment). Except for strips of linen or leather on their legs, they wore no body armor. A round or oval wooden shield, with a metal boss and support bars affixed to its center, provided their only defense. Their arms consisted of axes, lances, daggers, and swords.

Their favorite weapon was the *francisca*, an ax or hatchet to which they lent their name. Though they sometimes used it as a handheld weapon to strike blows, Franks became famous and feared for using it as a throwing ax. They also used a barbed lance or javelin called an *angon* for throwing from a distance or for spearing in close quarters. "In battle they hurl these javelins," wrote Greek historian Agathias (uh-GAY-thee-uhs), "and if they strike an enemy the barbs are so firmly fixed in his body that it is impossible to draw the weapon out."[9]

Frankish weapons of choice included a long sword, a short sword called a scramasax, and the infamous battle ax of the Franks, the francisca.

Up close, the Franks relied on daggers (actually short swords) and swords to finish off their enemies. The dagger or short sword was called a *scramasax*. It measured about twenty inches long and two inches wide and weighed two pounds. The sword—which was probably reserved for chiefs or elite soldiers—was thirty inches long. It had a flat, double-edged pointed blade and was carried in a wood or leather scabbard.

In a typical attack, the Franks would fill the air with flying axes and javelins to thin the ranks of their enemies, then close in for the kill with short swords. Few warriors in the Middle Ages surpassed the fury of the Franks in action.

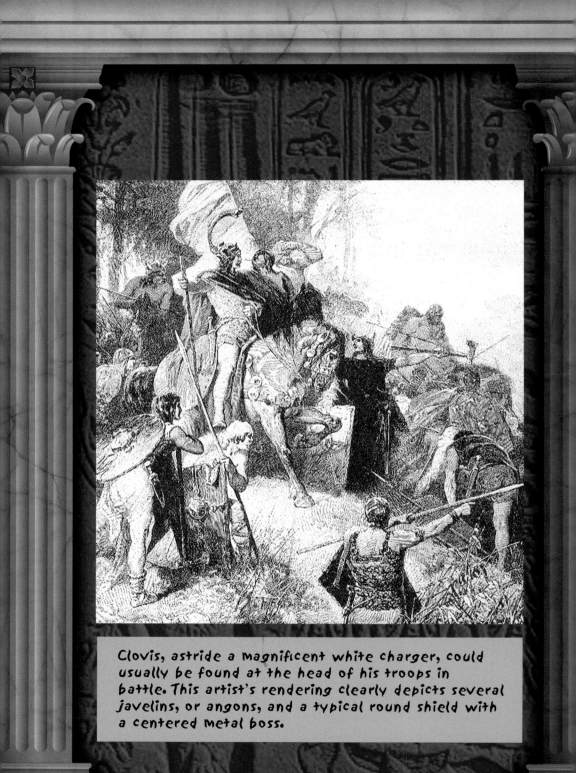

Clovis, astride a magnificent white charger, could usually be found at the head of his troops in battle. This artist's rendering clearly depicts several javelins, or angons, and a typical round shield with a centered metal boss.

BIOGRAPHY FROM ANCIENT CIVILIZATIONS
LEGENDS, FOLKLORE, AND STORIES OF ANCIENT WORLDS

CHAPTER
THREE

CLOVIS IN LOVE AND WAR

After his conquests in the Roman province of Belgica Secunda, Clovis continued to expand his kingdom. "He made many wars and gained many victories,"[1] wrote Gregory of Tours. Two of those victories came at the expense of his cousins Chararic and Ragnachar. The timeline of these events remains a subject for debate. Recent studies suggest that they occurred shortly after the defeat of Syagrius. Clovis probably wanted to remove any threat that his cousins might pose to his dominance over the Salian Franks. Moreover, both cousins had recently earned his displeasure. It seems logical that Clovis would act sooner rather than later.

Chararic had pledged to join Clovis in his battle against Syagrius. When the fighting began, however, he remained at a distance, waiting to see which side was winning before committing his forces. Clovis took his action—or lack of it—unkindly and marched against him. He caught up with Chararic and his son and imprisoned them both. Later, he issued orders to ordain Chararic as a priest and his son as a deacon. Chararic complained of his humiliation and wept. His son warned that they would both let their hair grow from their shaved heads like shoots from green wood. When their hair grew back, they would then kill the one responsible for their plight. Word of his threat soon reached Clovis. He ordered the beheading of both father and son. "When they were dead," noted Gregory of Tours, "he took their kingdom with the treasures and people."[2]

Clovis then turned to his other cousin, Ragnachar. Gregory described him as "a man so unrestrained in his wantonness that he scarcely had mercy for his own near relatives."[3] Ragnachar, it seems, shared a close relationship with his male counselor, Farro. Together, they engaged in vile behavior, sparing not even family members from their depravities. In time, the Franks of Cambrai grew outraged at the antics of their king. Clovis witnessed Ragnachar's errant conduct from a distance with contempt, but he needed a reason to take action against a relative. Ever resourceful, he contrived one: He bribed some of Ragnachar's vassals with fake gold trinkets for an invitation to intervene in their master's nasty behavior. Upon their invitation, Clovis marched on Ragnachar.

Clovis's army greatly outnumbered Ragnachar's forces and easily overwhelmed them. When Ragnachar realized he was beaten, he tried unsuccessfully to flee. His own soldiers quickly captured him, along with his brother, Ricchar. They bound the hands of both behind their backs and brought them before Clovis. "Why have you humiliated our family in permitting yourself to be bound?" Clovis asked. "It would have been better for you to die."[4] With that, he raised his ax and plunged it into his cousin's bowed head.

Ricchar looked on at his brother's execution. During the recently ended battle, he had acted as an observer rather than as a warrior. Clovis turned to him and said, "If you had aided your brother, he would not have been bound."[5] And with another swipe of his ax, he slew him as he had his sibling.

After Clovis had dispatched his cousins, Ragnachar's betrayers discovered that the gold trinkets they had received for their treachery were not gold but only gilded bronze. A spokesman for them approached Clovis to complain of the deception. Clovis pointed out that they should feel lucky that they, too, were not put to death. "Rightly," he said, "does he receive this [false] kind of gold, who of his own will brings his own master to death."[6] Gregory of Tours left their story with the betrayers pleading for their lives.

After the deaths of Ragnachar and Ricchar, only their brother Rignomer remained as Clovis's sole surviving relative and rival in northern Gaul. Rignomer ruled in Mans. Clovis ordered him slain in that city. "When they were dead," wrote Gregory, "Clovis received all their kingdom and treasures."[7] There were many ways to build an empire, and Clovis knew them all.

In 491, Clovis decided to add Thuringia to his kingdom. Aligning himself with Sigebert, chief of the Franks in neighboring Cologne (kuh-LOHN), Clovis attacked his mother's homeland. The Thuringians fought furiously but fell to the combined forces of the invaders in a battle that lasted about an hour. In the tenth year of his reign, Clovis had annexed another choice piece of land, further increasing his power.

Sometime during the next year—or perhaps a year later in 493—Clovis looked toward Burgundy that lay between southern Gaul and northern Italy. He might have had designs on the kingdom itself, but the fierce reputation of the Burgundians represented a need for caution. Means other than force might serve his interests better.

A king named Gundevech ruled in Burgundy. He apparently spent much of his time producing heirs—four sons named Gundobad, Godegisel, Chilperic, and Godomar. Gundobad cut a limb off the family tree, so to speak, by running his sword through his brother Chilperic. As further evidence of his sterling character, Gundobad sank his wife in water with a stone strung round her neck. Gundobad, who apparently was not much of a family man, continued to snip away at the family tree.

Gundobad's late brother Chilperic had two daughters, Chrona and Clotilda. Their uncle Gundobad sent them both off to exile. The eldest niece, Chrona, took the vows of chastity, poverty, and obedience and donned a nun's attire. Clotilda was found elsewhere in the kingdom by one of Clovis's envoys to Gundobad's court. These envoys, being good judges of maidenhood, reported to Clovis "that she was of good bearing and wise"[8] and of the family of Burgundy's king.

Clovis, intrigued, sent word to Gundobad, asking for Clotilda's hand in marriage. By then, he was ready to produce some heirs of his own. (Clovis already had a son named Theuderic out of wedlock.) Gundobad, fierce as he was, had no wish to find himself on the wrong side of the even fiercer Clovis. He consented to the marriage right away. When Clovis laid eyes on the beautiful Clotilda, it was love at first sight. "The king was very glad when he saw her, and married her,"[9] scribed Gregory of Tours. They took their vows sometime in 492 or 493.

The fair Clotilda was a Catholic. Her marriage to Clovis no doubt pleased the bishops and priests of the Roman Catholic clergy. They surely must have relished the idea of the young and brash chieftain of the powerful Franks taking a Catholic wife rather than one of pagan or Arian beliefs. At that time, Catholicism, paganism, and Arianism were vying for dominance in Western Europe. Clovis worshiped pagan gods but did not appear to be overly religious. He perhaps never considered the consequences of marrying someone of a different faith until Clotilda delivered a son.

Clotilda quite naturally wanted to have her son baptized and urged her husband to grant his consent. "The gods you worship are naught," she declared, "and can do naught for themselves or others; they are of wood, or stone, or metal."[10] In defense of his beliefs, Clovis answered, "It is by command of our gods that all things are created and brought forth. It is plain that your God hath no power; there is no proof even that he is of the race of gods."[11] While Clovis resisted, Clotilda went ahead with plans for her son's baptism. Her wishes prevailed, and their son was baptized and named Ingomer.

Right after being baptized, Ingomer died while still wearing the white garments of his christening. Clovis chastised his queen: "Had the child been dedicated to my gods he would be alive; he was baptized in the name of your God, and he could not live."[12] Clotilda defended her faith and prayed. "My soul is not stricken with grief for his sake, because I know that, summoned from this world as he was in his baptismal garments, he will be fed by the vision of God."[13]

In time, Clotilda bore Clovis a second son, who was also baptized as a Catholic. They named him Chlodomer. By some unfortunate quirk of fate, he too fell deathly ill. "It cannot be otherwise with him than with his brother," Clovis lamented; "baptized in the name of your Christ, he is going to die."[14] Again Clotilda prayed. This time, her son lived and grew strong. Two more sons and a daughter would follow—Childebert, Chlotar, and Clotilda (after her mother), respectively.

Clovis began to view his wife's God with less skepticism, but it would take more than the minor miracle of his son's recovery for him to renounce his own pagan religion. It would take an epiphany. That sudden awakening came to him on the field of battle.

Claiming Clotilda

Whether from lack of interest or information, Gregory of Tours skimmed over the details of how Clovis claimed Clotilda as his queen. Through the works of other chroniclers, a romantic myth has made its way through the ages. Briefly, it goes like this:

After hearing of Clotilda's beauty, Clovis sent a Roman friend named Aurelian to visit her secretly in Geneva. Disguised as a beggar, Aurelian carried a gold ring from his master with him. He presented it to Clotilda and told her that Clovis wanted her to share his throne. She said that they must seek permission from King Gundobad. Fearful that his refusal might anger the fierce king of the Franks, Gundobad gave his consent.

Soon afterward, Clotilda, urging great haste, returned to Gaul with Aurelian and some newly arrived escorts from Clovis. "I fear that the sage Aridius will return from Constantinople," she said, "and defeat our purpose." Now it seems that Aridius, Gundobad's chief minister, was due to return from a diplomatic mission at any time. She feared he would persuade Gundobad to rescind his permission. Her fears were realized.

Clotilda accepts a gold ring sent by Clovis, along with a proposal to become his queen.

Aridius returned from Constantinople and discovered what had recently occurred in his absence. Gundobad explained, "I have made a treaty of friendship with the Franks by giving Clovis my niece." His persuasive minister answered, "That is no treaty of friendship, but the seed of everlasting discord." He reminded the king that he had killed Chilperic, Clotilda's father, and other kin. "If she becomes powerful, she will avenge her kindred." Allegedly, Gundobad sent his troops racing after Clotilda, but too late. She made it safely to the Frankish kingdom, barely a step ahead of her pursuers.[15]

All this makes for an exciting tale—or perhaps more accurately, a *tall* tale. Scholars now believe that Gundobad did not murder his kin, thus Clotilda had no reason to seek revenge. As for Aurelian and Aridius, though they were real historical characters, little evidence suggests that they played a role in this scenario.

FYI For Your Info

In this page from a fifteenth-century illuminated manuscript, an angel sends a fleur-de-lis to Clovis at the time of his conversion to Catholicism in 496. By the twelfth century, the Capetian kings of France had adopted the stylized flower as a heraldic symbol, signifying that their authority came directly from God.

CHAPTER
FOUR

GOD AND CONQUEST

Though steadily pressured by Clotilda to renounce his pagan gods and convert to Catholicism, Clovis did not actively pursue Clotilda's Christian God. He did, however, pursue the Alemanni, and, in a manner of speaking, her God came to him. The Alemanni, like the Franks, were a confederation of Germanic tribes. They inhabited a region east of the upper Rhine, north of Switzerland, and had recently been assailing the Romans along their frontier. "From the source of the Rhine to its conflux with the Main and the Moselle, the formidable swarms of the Alemanni commanded either side of the river by the right of ancient possession or recent victory," wrote Edward Gibbon. "They had spread themselves into Gaul over the modern provinces of Alsace and Lorraine; and their bold invasion of the kingdom of Cologne summoned the Salic prince [Clovis] to the defence of his Ripuarian allies."[1] This occurred in 496 CE, the fifteenth year of Clovis's reign.

Gibbon goes on to state that Clovis clashed with the Alemanni on the plain of Tolbiac (or Tolbiacum; now Zülpich), near Cologne, and many succeeding historians concur. Recently, however, some scholars purport that the battle fought at Tolbiac was between the Alemanni and the Ripuarians, led by King Sigebert. The clash between Clovis and the Alemanni, they contend, more likely occurred somewhere in Alemanni territory. Apart from its location, most scholars agree that the battle's results significantly influenced the historic role of the Franks. Their victory established their power as being not only Gallic but also Germanic. (*Allemagne*, the French word for Germany, derives from the name of the Alemanni.) Clovis would likely be the first to say that his victory did not come easy.

In describing the Battle of Tolbiac (as the clash has become known), Gregory wrote: "It came about that as the two armies were fighting fiercely, there was much slaughter, and Clovis's army began to be in danger of destruction."[2] With his ax-wielding army teetering on the verge of collapse and defeat appearing all but inevitable, Clovis raised his eyes toward heaven and appealed to Clotilda's God. "I beseech the glory of thy aid," he cried, "with the vow that if thou wilt grant me victory over these enemies, and I shall know that power which she says that people dedicated in thy name have had from thee, I will believe in thee and be baptized in thy name."[3]

After this prayerful interlude, legend has it that Clovis personally led a charge that routed the Alemanni. They fled back across the Rhine,

In 496 CE, Clovis I and his Franks battled the Alemanni on the plains of Tolbiac, near Cologne. When the fighting turned against the Franks, Clovis called on God to help him reverse the tide of battle. Nineteenth-century artist Ary Scheffer immortalized that moment on canvas in 1837.

never to return. When they saw that their king had been slain, they offered themselves over to Clovis's dominion, saying: "Let not the people perish further, we pray; we are yours now."[4]

Like the people and the territories surrounding Soissons and the Belgic cities of Tongres and Cambrai, Clovis graciously assimilated the Alemanni and their lands into his kingdom. Thereafter, wrote Gibbon, "the Franks alone maintained their ancient habitations beyond the Rhine."[5] Theodoric the Great, the Ostrogoth king of Italy who had recently married Clovis's sister Albofleda, sent his congratulations. And lest Clovis might forget he owed his great victory to the Christian God, Clotilda stood close by his ear with frequent reminders of the divine intervention.

Clotilda took matters a step further. She implored St. Remigius (or St. Remi), bishop of Reims, to meet with Clovis secretly to urge his conversion to Catholicism. (Clotilda, it seems, believed that God helps those who help themselves.) Remi met secretly with Clovis to set him on the path to salvation. He urged the king to accept the one true God and renounce the many gods of his pagan heritage. Clovis, though receptive to his words, worried that his subjects might resist conversion. But he agreed to speak with his people.

Later, Clovis met with his followers. To his surprise, before he could speak, they cried out together: "O pious king, we reject our mortal gods, and we are ready to follow the immortal God whom Remi preaches."[6] Remi rejoiced upon hearing the news. He scheduled the momentous event for Christmas 496. Elaborate preparations began at once for the baptism of Clovis, his sisters Albofleda and Lanthechild, and more than three thousand of his warriors. In Reims, the clergy and laypeople shaded the squares with tapestried canopies, adorned the churches with white curtains, and readied the baptistery.

On Christmas Day, the king and his procession moved slowly down the road from the palace to the church. The clergy led the way, bearing the Holy Gospels, the Cross, and standards of the church and singing hymns and spiritual songs. Next in order came the bishop, leading Clovis by the hand. Clotilda followed close behind her king, and the rest of the procession trailed behind the queen. Ahead, at the church, the heavy aroma of incense mingled with the scent of brightly burning candles,

About 1500, a Franco-Flemish artist known as the Master of Saint Giles painted his conception of the conversion of Clovis to Christianity in 496. A bishop (probably Saint Remi) performs the baptismal ritual in The Baptism of Clovis, while Clotilda and others look on.

The fleur-de-lis (lily flower) is a stylized, three-petal version of a lily. It is said by some to have first been used by Clovis I to represent his God-given authority.

filling the entire shrine of the baptistery with nothing less than a divine fragrance.

Clovis asked first to be baptized, as was his kingly due, and Remi commenced the baptismal rites. As the king leaned his head over the baptismal font, the bishop cried, "Lower thy head with humility, Sicambrian [ancient Frank], adore what thou hast burned [the Cross]; burn what thou hast adored [pagan idols]."[7] The water of life poured through his long hair, cleansing his soul and offering him new life. He accepted the offer.

Clovis confessed to Clotilda's God in the Trinity, and Remi baptized him in the name of the Father, Son, and Holy Spirit. Albofleda and Lanthechild, some three thousand members of the Frankish army, and many women and children followed Clovis to the fountain that day and were similarly baptized. A short time later, Albofleda passed away. So wrote Gregory of Tours.

Word of Clovis's baptism spread swiftly across the land. Catholics celebrated. Accolades poured in to the Frankish court. Avitus, bishop of Vienne (vee-EN) and the chief prelate of the Burgundians, expressed his satisfaction in a note to Clovis: "Your faith is our victory; in choosing for you and yours, you have pronounced for all; divine Providence hath given you as arbiter to our age. Greece can boast of having a sovereign of our persuasion [Anastasius I]; but she is no longer alone in possession of this precious gift; the rest of the world doth share her light."[8]

Not to be outdone, Anastasius, the Byzantine emperor in Constantinople, hastened off this message: "The Church, our common mother, rejoiceth to have born unto God so great a king. Continue, glorious and illustrious son, to cheer the heart of this tender mother; be a column of iron to support her, and she in her turn will give thee victory over all thine enemies."[9] Now, as later events tend to bear out, Clovis might have turned such praise into a personal sense of invincibility. He was a man of high aims and did not wait long to test the Lord's favor and protection.

Clovis's conversion did little to allay his territorial aspirations. His next land grab came about by chance in 500 CE. At that time, Gundobad, Clotilda's uncle and murderer of her parents, ruled in the Burgundian region about the Rhône and the Saône (SOHN) rivers. His brother Godegisel reigned over the dependent principality of Geneva, but he wanted all of Burgundy for himself. He propositioned Clovis to help him kill Gundobad in an arranged battle. Godegisel promised to pay Clovis an annual tribute for his help. Clovis readily accepted the offer. At a prearranged time, Clovis and his army marched on Gundobad.

Gundobad, unaware of Godegisel's deception, called on his brother for help in repulsing the approaching Franks. Godegisel and his army set out from Geneva with a different purpose. The three armies collided at a stronghold named Dijon (dee-ZHON) on the Ouche (OOSH) River, 168 miles (270 kilometers) southeast of Paris. "While the Franks and Burgundians contended with equal valour," noted Gibbon, "[Godegisel's] seasonal desertion decided the event of the battle."[10] The combined armies of Clovis and Godegisel crushed Gundobad's forces. Gundobad fled the battlefield to seek safety in the city of Avignon (uh-vee-NYOH), some 250 miles (400 kilometers) to the south.

Clovis, victorious again, imposed an annual tribute on Gundobad and forced him to pardon his brother and reward his treachery. He then returned triumphantly to his own domain with the spoils of victory and captives of the southern provinces. Gundobad bided his time in defeat and eventually grew strong again. With restored strength, he attacked Godegisel and some five thousand Franks who had remained at Vienne. Gundobad ordered Godegisel and his fellow conspirators slain, but he spared the captive Franks by exiling them to King Alaric at Toulouse. He then reclaimed his dominion in Burgundy.

Clovis, perhaps grateful that Gundobad had spared his Franks, released him from tribute, and the two mended their relationship. Later, Clovis accepted "the alliance and military service of the king of Burgundy."[11] He would need Gundobad's help when he turned his vision of conquest southward to King Alaric and the Visigoths of Aquitania.

The New Constantine

In the time of Clovis, Christianity vied with Arianism for religious dominance in Europe. "Arianism, overcome within the [Roman] Empire," wrote popular historian Will Durant, "won a peculiar victory among the barbarians."[12] Many Goths accepted the Arian concept of Christianity. "As other barbarians received their Christianity in the fourth and fifth centuries from the Goths," Durant continued, "nearly all the invaders of the Empire were Arians."[13] Clovis, after converting to Christianity, became a virtual instrument of the church. Whether out of sincerity or for personal gain, he converted existing and subsequent subjects to his newly confessed religion. Gregory of Tours extolled him as the new Constantine.

Constantine I, the thirty-fourth Roman emperor, adopted Christianity as the religion of Rome. He fought against heresies (opinions opposed to church dogma) and heretics (proponents of heresies). Arius, a priest in Alexandria, posed a dissenting view of the nature of God. He rejected the orthodox Christian concept of God existing as three entities—the Father, the Son, and the Holy Spirit. Rather, he maintained that God is solely self-existent and immutable, that is, God exists as a single and absolute Divinity. His view of God thus reduced the Son to the status of a finite being of a different order of existence. Arianism, as the heresy became known, attracted many followers over the next several centuries.

In 325 CE, Constantine I convoked the Council of Nicaea (ny-SEE-uh) near Constantinople. The Council condemned Arius and his teachings and issued the Nicene Creed to safeguard the orthodox Christian belief. It states that the Son is *homoousion toi Patri* (of one substance with the Father). This declaration marked only the beginning of a long-drawn-out dispute. Some Germanic tribes clung to Arian beliefs through the seventh century. But those who fell under the sway of Clovis, the new Constantine, were converted.

Under the patronage of Roman emperor Constantine I, Christianity began to emerge as a world religion.

Clovis bids farewell to his devoted wife Clotilda and his infant son Chlodomer before the Battle of Tolbiac in 496. Dressed in full battle array, the helmeted king wears a linen tunic, a cloak and vest of fur, and leather shoes bound by leather thongs from ankles to knees. He carries an ax, a short sword, lance, a shield, and a javelin.

CHAPTER
FIVE

LEGENDS OF A WARRIOR KING

Clovis had long coveted the southern Gallic lands of Alaric II and the Visigoths of Aquitania. Like so many conquerors before and after him, however, he needed a proper pretext to launch an invasion. In religion, he appears to have found his excuse. By the turn of the century, many Gallic Catholics to the south were clamoring for relief from the oppressive Arian Visigoths. "Even at that time," chronicled Gregory of Tours, "many in the Gauls desired greatly to have the Franks as their masters."[1] Clovis was not opposed to becoming their savior. Neither was he inclined to refuse territory for the taking.

Further, from far-off Constantinople, Byzantine Emperor Anastasius I encouraged any action detrimental to his rival Theodoric the Great, Ostrogoth king of Italy. Theodoric was also the father-in-law of Alaric II and the brother-in-law of Clovis. He spent much of his time keeping the peace between his western in-laws. Anastasius would delight in any action that might disrupt or weaken his powerful Ostrogoth neighbor. Under these circumstances, whether divinely inspired or earthly motivated, the master of the Franks could not resist the lure of empire—particularly when the Lord willed it.

In 507 CE, Clovis assembled his top chieftains and said, "I take it very hard that these Arians hold part of the Gauls. Let us go with God's help and conquer them and bring their land under our control."[2] His words met their favor, and Clovis set his army in motion toward Poitiers, where Alaric happened to be staying at the time.

In one fabled incident along the way, Clovis forbade his soldiers to take anything from the land, except grass and water, when passing through the territory of Tours. He did so out of respect for St. Martin, a former bishop of Tours, and the future patron saint of France. One soldier disobeyed his edict and stole a bale of hay. When Clovis learned of his transgression, he said, "What will become of our hopes of victory, if we offend St. Martin?"[3] And with a single stroke of his sword, Clovis slew the offender.

Whether Clovis's defense of St. Martin's honor won him the favor of his Christian God cannot be known. It can be said, however, that the gods of war smiled upon his campaign against Alaric. Clovis led his army across the Loire and engaged Alaric's forces at Vouillé (or possibly Voulon), on the banks of the river Clain near Poitiers. The Franks chopped their way to advantage with their deadly short-handled axes—*franciscas*—and their king personally slew Alaric with his sword. "And

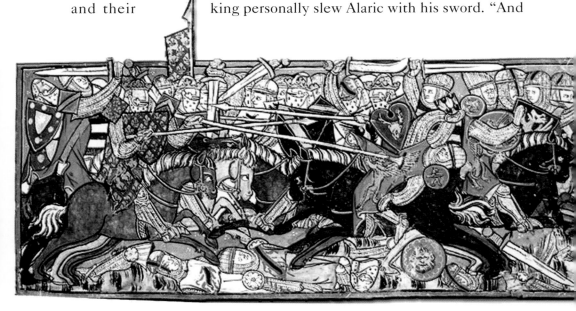

Clovis and his Franks won a great victory over Alaric II and his Visigoths at Vouillé in 507. An illustration from a medieval illuminated manuscript depicts battle tactics more in keeping with mounted knights with lances of a later era. Actually, Franks chopped their way to victory with their **franciscas.**

when the Goths had fled as was their custom," scribed Gregory, "king Clovis won the victory with God's aid."[4]

Clovis then ordered his oldest son, Theuderic, and a division of soldiers to cross central Gaul and link up with King Gundobad's army in Burgundy to the east. Gundobad had promised to help Clovis drive the remaining Visigoths from the banks of the Rhône and out of the southern province of Narbonensis. Theuderic acted boldly to carry out his father's orders, but Theodoric the Great intervened on behalf of his late son-in-law. With superior forces, Theodoric turned back Theuderic and his allies. In so doing, he thwarted the designs of Clovis and preserved the southeastern sector of Gaul for the Visigoths.

After this embarrassing setback, Clovis prudently decided to leave well enough alone and establish his authority in the territories he had already won. He first occupied Toulouse, then moved on to Bordeaux, and finally seized and occupied Angoulême, the only town of importance in Aquitania that he had not already conquered. In time, he returned to Tours, convinced that the Visigoths could or would not attempt to regain their lost lands. Perhaps in tribute to "God's aid," he scattered much captured gold and silver among the people lining the road from the church of the city to the church of St. Martin.

Clovis now ruled supreme over a Gallic domain that stretched as far south as Bordeaux and Toulouse. Even the Britons of Armorica in northeastern Gaul yielded their subordination and homage to Clovis. Despite his setback at the hands of Theodoric the Great, Clovis received the symbol of the consular dignity from an elated Emperor Anastasius in Constantinople. From then on, he proudly bore the name of consul, or *Augustus* (a title conferred upon Roman rulers).

After his sojourn in Tours, Clovis journeyed northward and established the seat of his kingdom in Paris. One last jewel remained to be set in his crown—the annexation of the Rhenish kingdom of Sigebert, king of the Ripuarian Franks in Cologne. His means of at last unifying all of the Franks gives pause to those of delicate senses. Legend proposes that Clovis pointed out the immediate benefits of inheritance to Sigebert's son, Chloderic, should his father die. "Of due right his kingdom would be yours," noted Clovis, "together with our friendship."[5]

Driven by greed, Chloderic ordered the assassination of his own father. After his henchmen had carried out his instructions, he sent word of the evil deed to Clovis. "My father is dead," wrote Chloderic, "and I have his treasures in my possession, and also his kingdom."[6] To seal their friendship, he asked Clovis to send men to collect a share of Sigebert's riches. Clovis readily complied. When Clovis's men arrived, Chloderic showed them Sigebert's chest filled with gold coins. They asked Chloderic to plunge his hand to the bottom of the chest to better reveal its contents. As he leaned forward to do so, one of Clovis's men raised his battle-ax and split Chloderic's skull.

An enduring legend holds that Clovis instigated the assassination of Sigebert by his son to acquire the Rhenish kingdom.

A short while later, Clovis arrived in Cologne from a boating excursion on the river Scheldt. He expressed his grief and outrage to the people at the slaying of his kinsmen. In a magnanimous gesture, he offered them his protection. The people listened, applauded, raised him upon their shields, and appointed him their king. Clovis added their kingdom and its treasures to his own. "For God was laying his enemies low every day under his hand, and was increasing his kingdom, because he walked with an upright heart before him, and did what was pleasing in his eyes."[7] In this way, all the Franks were united—or so the story goes.

In fairness to Clovis, some modern historians discount the foregoing tale as pure myth, fabricated by the wild imaginings of the barbarian mind. While conceding that Sigebert and Chloderic probably did die violently, they allow that the true circumstances of their earthly departures will remain forever unknown. Regardless of the manner of his succession, Clovis undeniably acquired the Ripuarian kingdom and united the Franks in the twenty-eighth year of his rule.

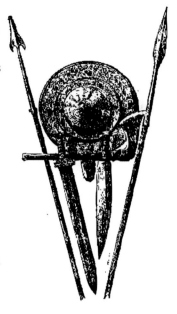

By the end of 509, with the integration of the Ripuarians and their lands, Clovis's kingdom had reached its apex. Returning to Paris, he exchanged his sword and shield for the trappings of his vast kingdom's chief administrator. He governed his many provinces by means of counts (*comites*) established in each city. Clovis personally selected every count from the aristocracy of Romans and barbarians to sustain the principle of absolute equality between both races. This principle dominated all his policies.

Sometime between 507 and 511, the Salic Law (*Lex Salica*) was committed to written form at Clovis's direction. In reducing it to the written word, scribes revised and updated it to conform to the emerging social conditions of Clovis's multiethnic subjects. Though primarily a penal and procedural code of the Salian Franks governing crimes and their punishment, the Salian Law also contained some civil law enactments. One famous passage of the law declared that daughters cannot inherit land. This declaration took on critical significance centuries later when incorrectly cited as authority for disallowing Henry II's granddaughter, Isabella of Spain, to assume the Valois crown.

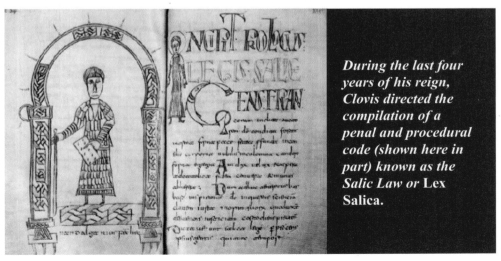

During the last four years of his reign, Clovis directed the compilation of a penal and procedural code (shown here in part) known as the Salic Law or Lex Salica.

The Education
of the Children
of Clovis (1861)
represents the
first major work
by nineteenth-
century Dutch
painter Sir
Lawrence
Alma-Tadema.
He depicts
Queen Clotilda
instructing
her children
in the fine art
of ax hurling,
supposedly to
avenge the death
of their father.

Clovis frequently acted to acknowledge the debt he owed to the clergy and the Church for their strong support over the tumultuous years. He recognized the Church as his kingdom's most civilizing influence and went to great lengths to protect it. In 511, he instituted the National Council of Orléans. There the bishops of Gaul resolved a range of problems dealing with relations between Church and state. And if legendary claims hold true, he founded innumerable churches and monasteries across his kingdom.

Clovis, a warrior old and worn at the age of forty-five, died on November 27, 511. He was interred in the Church of the Holy Apostles (later of Ste. Geneviève) that he and Clotilda had built to the south of Paris. "Queen Clotilda came to Tours after the death of her husband and served there in the church of St. Martin," wrote Gregory, "and dwelt in the place with the greatest chastity and kindness all the days of her life, rarely visiting Paris."[8] She joined her husband in the Church of Ste. Geneviève some thirty-four years after his passing.

Founder of France

At the dawning of the Middle Ages, no monarch stood taller in Western Europe than the towering figure of Clovis, king of the Franks. Lionized in poetry and denigrated in myth, the character of Clovis defies accurate appraisal. Without regard to his personal makeup, history recalls him best for three achievements: his unification of the Frankish tribes; his conquest of Gaul; and his conversion to Roman Catholicism.

Clovis was demonstrably a superior strategist, an astute tactician, and a ferocious warrior. His prowess in battle made him famous and feared in his time. Through the lens of history, his warrior skills have also obscured his considerable talents as an organizer, a statesman, and an administrator. He built an empire on the ruins of a fallen Rome, created a system founded on equality for all, and governed fairly. Out of the empire that Clovis shaped sprang the modern nations of France, Germany, Belgium, the Netherlands, and Luxembourg. His name and variations of it—Louis, and others—lived on in a long line of European rulers, including a Holy Roman emperor. Not bad for a barbarian.

As was the custom of his time and place, when Clovis passed, his Merovingian kingdom was divided among his four sons, Theuderic I (Reims), Chlodomer I (Orléans), Childebert I (Paris), and Chlotar I (Soissons). The Merovingian dynasty—founded by his father Childeric but raised to prominence and power by Clovis— endured for about 275 years. A pattern of divided rule and continual internal bickering eventually brought down the house that Clovis built.

In 750, Pippin III the Short deposed the last Merovingian ruler, Childeric III, and ushered in the Carolingian dynasty. The world remembers his famous son, Charlemagne, as the great Carolingian king of the Franks. But the French will honor Clovis evermore as the founder of France.

Clovis I sits on his throne wearing a royal robe with fleurs-de-lis, emblematic of the authority granted to him by God.

For Your Info

CHRONOLOGY

c.466	Clovis is born
481	Succeeds his father, Childeric, as ruler of the Salian Franks of Tournai
486	Defeats Syagrius, the last Roman governor, at the battle of Soissons
c.492–493	Marries Clotilda, the niece of Gundobad, the king of the Burgundians
494	Establishes Frankish dominion over most of northern Gaul
496	Conquers the Alemanni at Tolbiacum (Zülpich), near Cologne; baptized as a Catholic Christian by St. Remigius, bishop of Reims, on Christmas Day
500	Defeats the Burgundians at Dijon
507	Vanquishes the Visigoths at Vouillé (or possibly Voulon) near Poitiers
c.507–511	Issues Salic Law (*Lex Salica* in Latin), the code of the Salian Franks
509	Acquires the Ripuarian kingdom and unites all the Franks
511	Institutes National Council of Orléans; dies in Paris on November 27. His kingdom is divided among his four sons: Theuderic, Chlodomer, Childebert, and Chlotar

395	The Roman Empire splits into East and West.
410	Alaric, king of the Visigoths, invades and sacks Rome. Roman legions are withdrawn from Britain to defend Italy.
411	St. Augustine writes *City of God* after the sack of Rome by Alaric in 410.
416	The Visigoths conquer the Vandal kingdom in Spain.
420	Nanking is restored as the capital of northern China.
425	Constantinople University is founded.
429	Gaiseric, king of the Vandals, founds kingdom in northern Africa. Roman general Aetius, chief minister of Valentinian III, becomes the virtual ruler of the Western Roman Empire.
432	St. Patrick embarks on his mission to Ireland.
433	Attila becomes co-ruler of the Huns with his brother Bleda.
442	Galla Placida, daughter of Eastern Roman Emperor Theodosius the Great, erects her famous Mausoleum at Ravenna.
450	Marcian succeeds Theodosius II as emperor of the Eastern Roman Empire.
452	Venice is founded by refugees from Attila's Huns.
453	Attila the Hun dies.
470	Huns withdraw from Europe.
476	Western Roman Empire falls.
500	First plans for the Vatican Palace are drafted in Rome. Incense is introduced in Christian church services.
517	Chinese Emperor Wu-Ti embraces Buddhism and introduces the new religion to southern China.
527	Reconstruction begins on the Church of the Nativity in Jerusalem; it will be completed in 565.
529	Byzantine Emperor Justinian I issues Code of Civil Laws—the *Codex Vetus*.
539	War breaks out between Byzantine Empire and Persia; it will end in 562.
540	Totila, future king of the Ostrogoths, ends Byzantine rule in Italy.
552	Christian missionaries return to Constantinople with silkworms from China and Ceylon; European silk industry begins. Emperor Shotoko Taishi introduces Buddhism to Japan.
558	Chlotar I, son of Clovis, reunites the kingdom of the Franks.
570	Mohammed, founder of Islam, is born.

Chapter One. "A Great and Distinguished Warrior"

1. Medieval Sourcebook: Gregory of Tours: *On Clovis*, http://www.fordham.edu/halsall/source/gregtours1.html, p. 1
2. Ibid.
3. Ibid.
4. Ibid.
5. Ibid.
6. Ibid.
7. Ibid.
8. Edward Gibbon, *The Decline and Fall of the Roman Empire* (Vols. 40 and 41/ Gibbon I and II, *Great Books of the Western World*. Robert Maynard Hutchins, Editor in Chief. Chicago: Encyclopaedia Britannica, 1952), I, p. 103.
9. Ibid.
10. Francois P. G. Guizot, *Clovis Founds the Kingdom of the Franks: It Becomes Christian*, http://history-world.org/franks.htm, p. 3.
11. Medieval Sourcebook: Gregory of Tours (539–594): *History of the Franks*: Books I–X, http://www.fordham.edu/halsall/basis/gregory-hist.html, p. 30.
12. Ibid.
13. Joseph Dahmus, *A History of the Middle Ages* (New York: Barnes & Noble, 1995), p. 106.

Chapter Two. King of the Salian Franks

1. Edward Gibbon, *The Decline and Fall of the Roman Empire* (Vols. 40 and 41/ Gibbon I and II, *Great Books of the Western World*. Robert Maynard Hutchins, Editor in Chief. Chicago: Encyclopaedia Britannica, 1952), I, p. 581.
2. Ibid.

3. Medieval Sourcebook: Gregory of Tours (539–594): *History of the Franks*: Books I–X, http://www.fordham.edu/halsall/basis/gregory-hist.html, p. 31.
4. Ibid., p. 32.
5. Gibbon, p. 609.
6. Ibid., p. 610.
7. Joseph Dahmus, *A History of the Middle Ages* (New York: Barnes & Noble, 1995), p. 199.
8. Gibbon, pp. 609–10.
9. Charles Oman, *A History of the Art of War in the Middle Ages* (Volume One: 378–1278 CE. Mechanicsburg, PA: Stackpole Books, 1998), p. 52.

Chapter Three. Clovis in Love and War

1. Medieval Sourcebook: Gregory of Tours (539–594): *History of the Franks*: Books I–X, http://www.fordham.edu/halsall/basis/gregory-hist.html, p. 33.
2. Ibid., p. 39.
3. Ibid.
4. Ibid.
5. Ibid.
6. Ibid.
7. Ibid.
8. Ibid., p. 33.
9. Ibid.
10. Francois P. G. Guizot, *Clovis Founds The Kingdom of the Franks: It Becomes Christian*, http://history-world.org/franks.htm, p. 9.
11. Ibid.
12. Ibid.
13. Medieval Sourcebook: Gregory of Tours, p. 33.
14. Guizot, p. 9.
15. Northvegr Foundation: *The Invasion of Europe by the Barbarians*, http://www.northvegr.org/lore/bury/026.php, p. 2.

Chapter Four.
God and Conquest

1. Edward Gibbon, *The Decline and Fall of the Roman Empire* (Vols. 40 and 41/ Gibbon I and II, *Great Books of the Western World*. Robert Maynard Hutchins, Editor in Chief. Chicago: Encyclopaedia Britannica, 1952), I, p. 610.

2. Medieval Sourcebook: Gregory of Tours (539–594): *History of the Franks*: Books I–X, http://www.fordham.edu/halsall/basis/gregory-hist.html, p. 34.

3. Ibid.

4. Ibid.

5. Gibbon, p. 611.

6. Medieval Sourcebook: Gregory of Tours, p. 34.

7. Francois P. G. Guizot, *Clovis Founds the Kingdom of the Franks: It Becomes Christian*, http://history-world.org/franks. htm, p. 11.

8. Ibid.

9. Ibid.

10. Gibbon, p. 612.

11. Ibid., p. 613.

12. Will Durant, *The Age of Faith: A History of Medieval Civilization—Christian, Islamic, and Judaic—from Constantine to Dante: A.D. 325–1300* (Vol. 4, The Story of Civilization. New York: Simon and Schuster, 1950), p. 46.

13. Ibid., p. 47.

Chapter Five.
Legends of a Warrior King

1. Medieval Sourcebook: Gregory of Tours (539–594): History of the Franks: Books I–X, http://www.fordham.edu/halsall/basis/gregory-hist.html, p. 36.

2. Ibid.

3. Francois P. G. Guizot, *Clovis Founds the Kingdom of the Franks: It Becomes Christian*, http://history-world.org/franks. htm, p. 12.

4. Medieval Sourcebook: Gregory of Tours, p. 37.

5. Ibid., p. 38.

6. Ibid.

7. Ibid.

8. Ibid., p. 39.

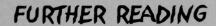

FURTHER READING

For Young Adults

Greenblatt, Miriam. *Charlemagne and the Early Middle Ages.* Tarrytown, NY: Marshall Cavendish, 2002.

Jett, Stephen C., and Lisa Roberts. *France.* New York: Chelsea House Publishers, 2003.

Knoell, Donna L. *France.* Mankato, MN: Capstone Press, 2002.

Sypeck, Jeff. *The Holy Roman Empire and Charlemagne in World History.* Berkeley Heights, NJ: Enslow Publishers, 2002.

Works Consulted

Boutell, Charles. *Arms and Armour in Antiquity and the Middle Ages.* Conshohocken, PA: Combined Books, 1996.

Burns, Thomas S. *Rome and the Barbarians, 100 B.C.–A.D. 400.* Baltimore: The Johns Hopkins University Press, 2003.

Cantor, Norman F. *The Civilization of the Middle Ages.* New York: HarperCollins Publishers, 1993.

Cantor, Norman F. (editor). *The Encyclopedia of the Middle Ages.* New York: Viking, 1999.

Currier, John W. *Clovis, King of the Franks.* Milwaukee, WI: Marquette University Press, 1997.

Dahmus, Joseph. *A History of the Middle Ages.* New York: Barnes & Noble, 1995.

Daniels, Patricia S., and Stephen G. Hyslop. *Almanac of World History.* Washington, DC: National Geographic Society, 2003.

Davies, Norman. *Europe: A History.* New York: Oxford University Press, 1996.

Delbrück, Hans. *Medieval Warfare. Vol. 3, History of the Art of War.* Translated by Walter J. Renfroe, Jr. Lincoln: University of Nebraska Press, 1990.

Dupuy, R. Ernest, and Trevor N. Dupuy. *The Encyclopedia of Military History from 3500 B.C. to the Present.* Revised Edition. New York: Harper & Row, Publishers, 1977.

Durant, Will. *The Age of Faith: A History of Medieval Civilization—Christian, Islamic, and Judaic—from Constantine to Dante: A.D. 325–1300. Vol. 4, The Story of Civilization.* New York: Simon and Schuster, 1950.

Gibbon, Edward. *The Decline and Fall of the Roman Empire.* Vols. 40 and 41/Gibbon I and II, *Great Books of the Western World.* Robert Maynard Hutchins, Editor in Chief. Chicago: Encyclopaedia Britannica, 1952.

Lopez, Robert S. *The Birth of Europe.* New York: M. Evans and Company, 1967.

Oman, Charles. *A History of the Art of War in the Middle Ages. Volume One: 378–1278 CE.* Mechanicsburg, PA: Stackpole Books, 1998.

On the Internet

Guizot, Francois P. G. *Clovis Founds the Kingdom of the Franks: It Becomes Christian* http://history-world.org/franks.htm

Medieval Sourcebook: Gregory of Tours (539–594): *History of the Franks*: Books I–X http://www.fordham.edu/halsall/basis/gregory-hist.html

Medieval Sourcebook: Gregory of Tours: *On Clovis* http://www.fordham.edu/halsall/source/gregtours1.html

Northvegr Foundation: *The Invasion of Europe by the Barbarians* http://www.northvegr.org/lore/bury/026.php

GLOSSARY

angon (ahn-ZHAHN)—A barbed lance or javelin used for throwing or for spearing in close quarters.

annexation (an-ek-SAY-shun)—The adding of a territory to the domain of a larger state or empire.

Arian (AYR-ee-en)—An early variant branch of Christianity; it advocated that God alone is God, and that the Son is not of the same substance as the Father but was created as an agent for creating the world.

Campus Martius (KAM-pus MAR-shuhs)—Latin for "Field of Mars"; originally the floodplain of the Tiber River used for Roman military exercises; later applied to other broad, open areas used for similar purposes.

foederati (fed-uh-RAH-tee)—Latin for "federated allies"; barbarians who fought as allies or mercenaries under their own leaders in Roman service.

francisca (fran-SIS-kuh)—An ax or hatchet used as a handheld weapon for striking blows or as a throwing ax.

Gaul (gawl)—A medieval country with varying boundaries, out of which emerged the modern nations of France, Germany, Belgium, the Netherlands, and Luxembourg.

heathen (HEE-then)—A person who does not believe in the God of the Bible.

heresy (HAYR-uh-see)—A religious opinion that is contrary to the orthodox doctrine or accepted beliefs of a particular religion.

metal boss (MET-al baws)—A round projecting knob or stud made of metal.

pagan (PAY-gun)—One who worships many gods or none; a heathen.

prelate (PREH-lit)—A cleric of superior rank, such as a bishop or abbot.

regulus (REG-yuh-luhs); plural: *reguli*—Derived from a Latin word for "king"; a tribal chieftain or leader.

scramasax (SKRAH-muh-saks)—A dagger or short sword.

INDEX